SISTER WENDY'S
──── BOOK OF ────
MEDITATIONS

SISTER WENDY'S
BOOK OF
MEDITATIONS

[DK]
DORLING KINDERSLEY
LONDON · NEW YORK · SYDNEY · MOSCOW

A DORLING KINDERSLEY BOOK

Editors *Lara Maiklem,*
Patricia Wright
Senior Art editor *Claire Legemah*
Senior editor *Luci Collings*
Managing editor *Anna Kruger*
Deputy art director *Tina Vaughan*
Picture researcher *Jo Walton*
Production controllers *Alex Bertram,*
Alison Jones

First published in Great Britain in 1998 by
Dorling Kindersley Limited
9 Henrietta Street, London WC2E 8PS

A CIP catalogue record for this book is available from
the British Library.

ISBN 075131123 5

CONTENTS

Colour reproduction by Mullis Morgan.
Printed and bound in Italy by Garzanti Verga.

· MEDITATIONS ON LOVE ·

· MEDITATIONS ON JOY ·

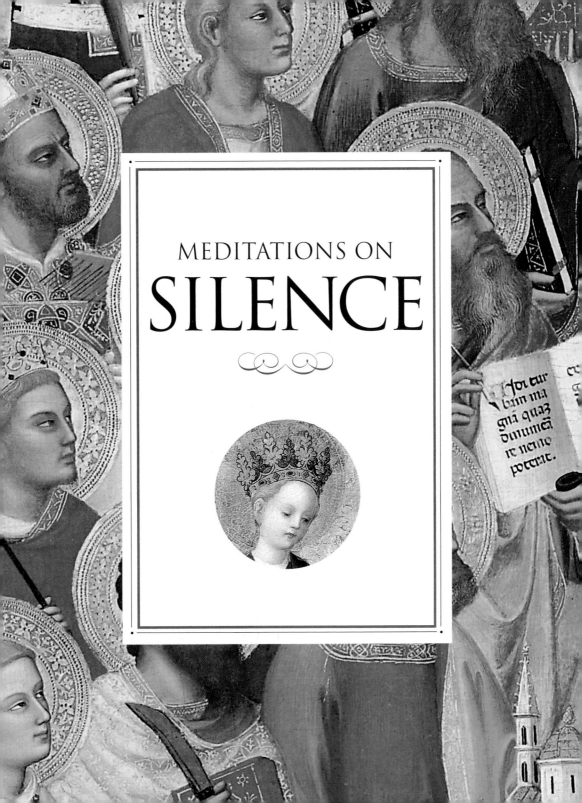

MEDITATIONS ON
SILENCE

PROFOUND SILENCE

THE CAPACITY FOR SILENCE – a deep, creative awareness of one's inner truth – is what distinguishes us as human. All of us, however ordinary or flawed, have at heart a seemingly boundless longing for fulfilment, and it is their consciousness of this that makes Rembrandt's portraits so beautiful. The *Woman with a Pink* is lost in the depths of her private reflections. Her dark background is symbolically unimportant, lending greater expression to the soft brightness that plays upon her face. Visibly silent, she is explicitly encountering the mystery of being human. She does not contemplate the carnation (the "pink"), usually an emblem of love, but looks within, in silence, quiet and engrossed.

Woman with a Pink, 1665-9, Rembrandt Van Rijn
92 x 74.5 cm (36¼ x 29¼ in) oil on canvas
Metropolitan Museum of Art, New York

RELATIVE SILENCE

PERUGINO'S FACES ARE often too sweet, too other-worldly, but this little picture is unforgettable. It is only in the most technical sense *St Mary Magdalen*, and Perugino has blazoned her name in embroidered capitals across her tunic as if in wry recognition of this. What she is is a young girl, silent indeed, but as yet unprepared to accept the seriousness of living inwardly. She floats on the surface of her spirit, pensive but not committed. This is so relative a silence that it has little transformative power. It is that easy silence, of which the most accessible form is the daydream. Real silence is both supremely simple and yet not easy. It draws us into a dimension always open to those who will allow themselves to be centred. But centring debars us from many irrelevances in which we take a guilty pleasure: Perugino's little beauty is not yet ready for the light.

St Mary Magdalen (cropped), c.1500, Pietro Perugino
47 x 34 cm (18^1/$_2$ x 13^1/$_2$ in), oil on wood panel
Pitti Palace, Florence

S MARIA MADALENA

A WAY THROUGH

LIFE SEEMS SIMPLER if we blot out awareness of its mystery, but such a life is an impoverished one. There is a dimension to ourselves, the most essential dimension, which it is folly to ignore. Patricia Wright's *Gate* is a delicate image of this. She shows us the complexities of a normal existence – lines in confusion, with hints of gridded order behind, to which we are not privy. As we move to the centre, the lines grow ever more clotted and chaotic: who can ever understand the meaning of events that make up our conscious experience – in relationships, in business, or whatever? But the swirls of events are the context wherein is held the gate. It is a real but shadowy presence, a way through, a possibility. If we allow silence to open up within, we shall see the gate and be free to open it.

Gate, 1993, Patricia Wright
23 x 23 cm (9 x 9 in), acrylic on paper
Private collection

INTO THE LIGHT

THE GATE THAT SILENCE opens up within us leads to light. Light exposes with an almost merciless radiance and, in the exposure, reveals the beauty of the real. Vermeer always painted this holy light. He may seem, on first looking, to be depicting a young woman, standing at a half-opened window, wrapped peacefully in her own thoughts, but she and her surroundings are merely the pretext. Vermeer's intensity is focused on the light itself, only visible to us as it falls on the material world. It shimmers on the woman's white headdress, glimmers on the copper of the jug and ewer, gleams with ineffable softness on the walls. Every element in the painting celebrates the presence of light, revealing and transforming. No painter has ever believed more totally in light than Vermeer – and hence the profoundly contemplative nature of his art.

Young Woman with a Water Jug, c.1662, Jan Vermeer
46 x 42 cm (17⁷/8 x 16¹/2 in), oil on canvas
Metropolitan Museum of Art, New York

MANIFESTATION

ONLY THE ABSTRACT artist can attempt to show us light in itself, free from any material context. This is pure silence, the experience removed from the concrete and celebrated as a transforming peace. Epiphany is a Greek word meaning manifestation, a revelation of glory. We are not meant to understand Natkin's picture, any more than we are meant to intellectualise during our silences. We enter into silence to let the holiness of mystery take possession of us. We do this not in the absence of thought, but beneath thought. Natkin shows us infinite shades of colour, a constantly receding radiance. The longer that we gaze at it, the more we "see": not in understandable images but in pure experience of chromatic brightness. This undifferentiated experience is integral to silence.

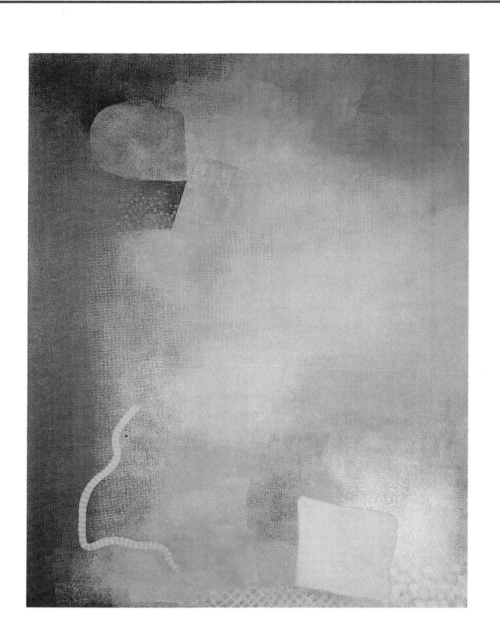

Epiphany, 1990, Robert Natkin
178 x 127 cm (70 x 50 in), acrylic on canvas
Private collection

THE STILL MIND

WHAT MATTERS IS not silence itself, which can be merely physical, but what we do within it. The great mystic, Teresa of Avila, called the mind a clacking mill that goes on grinding. This is the nature of the mind: to have thoughts. We can indeed still the mind, through intense psychic application, but such application – directed wholly to the self – may be so self-satisfying as to abnegate its very purpose. The purpose of silence is a directed stillness, which receives rather than acts. There is only one state of perfect freedom from thought, and that is ecstasy. Raphael's St Catherine is rapt, lost to everything but her comprehension of God. She leans carelessly on the wheel of her martyrdom, which curves inexorably towards the heavens where she truly lives. This rapturous state is pure gift and not for our seeking. (As soon as we seek, self comes in and renders the whole thing useless.)

St Catherine of Alexandria (cropped), c.1507, Raphael
71.5 x 53.5 cm (28 x 21¾ in), oil on wood panel
National Gallery, London

A RICH EMPTINESS

EN JOHNSON HAS taken as his special theme the way light shines on emptiness. *The Queen's House, Greenwich* is utterly still, utterly bare to our gaze. We are presented with a silent vista, not so much an invitation to advance through the arch and onwards as to stand motionless and simply experience. There is almost tangibly no sound, and what Johnson manages to suggest, implicitly, is that the richness is in the standing still, the non-acting. Just to be there, to take our smallness into this classical poise, is to become more potentially our true selves; it is not outer reality that silence reveals, but our own innerness. Silence is essentially a surrender to the holiness of the divine mystery, whether we use these words or not. An atheist, calming his or her spirit in the peace of silence, is irradiated by the same mystery, anonymous but transforming. We are to listen. To what? To silence.

Queen's House, Greenwich II, 1978, Ben Johnson
244 x 120 cm (96 x 47$\frac{1}{4}$ in), acrylic on canvas
Private collection

MEDITATIVE SILENCE

THERE ARE LAYERS of silence. Van der Weyden's Magdalen is deeply silent, but she is reading. Her mind is active, and willed into activity. This, then, is a mitigated silence, since we are only receptive to the thoughts of what we are reading. The Magdalen is obviously reading the scriptures, and meditating on what she reads, but her silence can only be between passages of reading and will be concerned with those passages. If we do not read with intervals of silent reflection, we will understand only in part what we read. This is a fractured silence, good but imperfect. We all need to read, to keep our spirit alert, to have an inner texture, as it were, that can respond to the absolutes of pure soundlessness, but this chosen, meditative layer, is the least significant.

The Magdalen Reading (detail), c.1445, Rogier Van der Weyden
61.5 x 54.5 cm (24¹/₄ x 21¹/₂ in), oil on wood panel
National Gallery, London

A PARADOX

SILENCE IS A PARADOX, intensely "there" and, with equal intensity, "not there". The passivity of silence is hard to explain, since in one respect it is intensely active. We hold ourselves in a condition of surrender. We choose not to initiate, nor to cooperate with our mental processes. Yet from this passivity arises creativity. This mysterious liberation from all commonplace worldly demands is exemplified in

Rebecca Salter's abstractions, which have been compared to gazing at a waterfall. Salter seems as if to have painted silence itself: the work is both alive and moving, and yet still, so that the eye wanders absorbed and yet patternless, through and among the shapes before us. There is nothing to say, nothing even to experience in any words that sound impressive, yet the looking never wearies. This is a rough image, in

its very imagelessness, of the bliss of silence.

Untitled H30 (diptych), 1993
Rebecca Salter
137 x 244 cm (54 x 96 in)
Acrylic and canvas
Jill George Gallery, London

Desiring Silence

PROFOUND SILENCE IS NOT something we fall into casually. This may indeed happen, and a blessed happening it is, but normally we choose to set aside a time and a place to enter into spiritual quietness. (Those who never do this, or shrink from it, run a very grave risk of remaining half-fulfilled as humans). Craigie Aitchison's view of Holy Island pares this choice down to its fundamental simplicities. Brown earth, blue sea, red sky, Holy Island a stony grey lit by glory. There is a small ship to take us across, if we choose to ride in it. There are no fudging elements here: all is clear-cut. This is not silence itself but rather the desire for silence. Silence, being greater than the human psyche, cannot be compressed within our intellectual categories; it will always escape us. But the desire to be silent, the understanding of the absolute need for it: this is expressed in Aitchison's wonderful diagram of life within the sight of the holy.

Holy Island from Lamlash, 1994, Craigie Aitchison
106.5 x 96.5 cm (42 x 38 in), oil on canvas
Thomas Gibson Fine Art Ltd, London

CLEANSING

NTERING INTO SILENCE is like stepping into cool clear water. The dust and debris are quietly washed away, and we are purified of our triviality. This cleansing takes place whether we are conscious of it or not: the very choice of silence, of desiring to be still, washes away the day's grime. Courbet's soft-flowing stream disappears into the darkness of the cliff, a happy image of the mystery to which we surrender ourselves when we accept the balm of silence.

The River Brême, 1865, Gustave Courbet
73.5 x 92.5 cm (29 x 36¹/2 in), oil on canvas
Musée des Beaux-Arts et d'Archéologie Besançon

TRUE PERSPECTIVE

OUR WORLD MAY BE one of struggle or even combat. It was at the Battle of Issus that Alexander the Great changed the course of the then-world's history, yet how small and remote it is in Altdorfer's painting. We are above it all, distanced by the immensities of time and space, looking down from a heavenly height at the tiny passions of those who fight. From here even the mountains seem small and inconsiderable, and the only real event is in the skies, where light encounters darkness – the daily and fore-destined battle we call dawn and sunset. Silence, distancing us, shakes our life into perspective, and we learn not to care for what is ephemeral and insignificant.

The Battle of Issus (detail), 1529, Albrecht Altdorfer
158.5 x 120.5 cm (62¹/₂ x 47¹/₂ in), oil on wood panel
Alte Pinakothek, Munich

AMID THE CHAOS

TO KNOW WHAT matters and what does not is the lesson
that we long to be taught. Mondrian's *Still Life with Ginger
Pot II* shows us a geometrical tangle of incoherent lines,
which might or might not have a meaning. But at the centre of
all this, pure, rounded, and still, gleams the pot, the one satisfying

Still Life with Ginger Pot II, 1911-12, Piet Mondrian
91.5 x 120 cm (36 x 47¹/4 in), oil on canvas
Haags Gemeentemuseum, The Hague

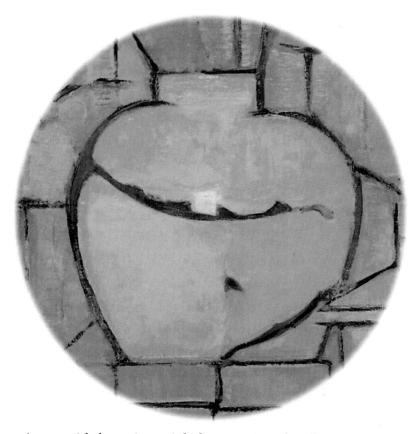

certainty amid the existential chaos. It is only when we are still, when we open up to our inner reality that the things in our life fall into coherence for us. We do not necessarily have to think this out: silence makes the order plain. But instead we quieten our restless minds, and then rise to find that we see now, the essential.

SILENCE AND TIME

A QUICK GLANCE AT *Three Greys* and we might walk away, thinking it drab and over-regulated. A slower glance, and the painting reveals an infinitude of subtle hues and shifting verticals. Its beauty, like so much else we see, reveals itself only in time. Silence is making-friends-with-time. It does not fight it or waste it, it refuses to run after it. Silence floats free with time, letting the pattern of the moments unfold at its own pace. It is a way of becoming free, not only for the practical advantage of being able to "see" the beauty in what is grey, for example, but at a far deeper level. In silence we break the hold time has on us, and accept in practice that our true home is in eternity.

Three Greys, 1987, Yuko Shiraishi
183 x 137 cm (72 x 54 in), oil on canvas
Edward Totah Gallery, London

FORTITUDE

OTTICELLI'S LOVELY *Fortitude* is armed: she maintains a waiting silence. This is silence as attentiveness, a gathering together of one's forces. *Fortitude* is not in the least on the attack. She sits amidst her flowing drapery and holds her weapon at rest. But she is alert in her resting. Her feet are poised to spring into action and her arms and bosom are protected by armour. There is nothing casual about silence. In its peace it is productive. It prepares us for whatever is to come. Our bodily eyes may (or may not) be shut, but the eyes of the spirit are wide-open and watchful. Silence is, in itself, an armour.

Fortitude, c.1470, Sandro Botticelli
167 x 87 cm (65³/₄ x 34¹/₄ in), tempera on wood panel
Uffizi Gallery, Florence

BEYOND BABEL

WHAT SILENCE principally armours us against is Babel: the endless foolish chatter, words used to confound thought, words misused to ward off friendship or attachments, words as occupation. The biblical Babel was a metaphor for the loss of human ability to communicate as a consequence of the rise of different languages; but the foreignness of other tongues is a smokescreen. To express what one means, and to hear what another means: this is a rare thing. Babel is profoundly destructive of our energies, as Bruegel so splendidly shows. This monstrous tower is consuming all who labour on or near it. We have an absolute need for quiet, for the heart's wordless resting on God.

The Tower of Babel, c.1563, Pieter Bruegel the Elder
114 x 155 cm (44¹/2 x 61 in), tempera on wood panel
Kunsthistoriches Museum, Vienna

A STILL LIFE

IN A CRYSTAL VASE, bathed in sunlight, Manet's *White Lilac* has no function except to exist. In the last year of his life, wretchedly shortened through illness, Manet painted several of these vases of simple flowers. Their singleness of being must have moved him and perhaps consoled him, amidst the anxieties and anguishes of his own pain-filled days. Silence has something of this function: a simplifying, a beautifying. It reminds us that we have only to be still and let the waters of grace refresh us and the sunlight of peace shine upon us.

White Lilac, 1882-3, Edouard Manet
54 x 42 cm (21¹/₄ x 16¹/₂ in), oil on canvas
National Gallery, Berlin

AWAITING SILENCE

THIS ENCHANTING miniature shows a young woman, alone in the night, awaiting her lover. All nature seems to wait with her, and the moon swings in the sky like an expectant hammock. It is this confident expectation that makes silence possible. We are actively waiting. What (or whom) we are waiting for must be a personal recognition that each must make alone. But silence is only possible if we trust in it.

Awaiting the Beloved, 1820-25, Indian miniature
25 x 17cm (10 x 6 3/4 in), gouache on paper
Victoria and Albert Museum, London

THE BLISS OF SILENCE

THIS TILE STOOD for centuries on the ridge of the roof of a Chinese temple or perhaps home. It shows a Lohan, a Buddhist saint, a monk who has "made it": attained pure bliss. Weather-beaten by all the seasons, this Lohan expresses most beautifully the bliss of silence. He has that inner smile that tells of an immensity of peace. His silence has been totally fruitful; he has found true fulfilment. He smiles, not at us, nor for any specific purpose, but because his quiet has brought him to this state of gentle smiling. He is where we desire silence one day to bring us all.

Buddhist Ridgetile, China,
Late Ming dynasty
38 cm (15 in), glazed pottery
Alistair Sampson Ltd

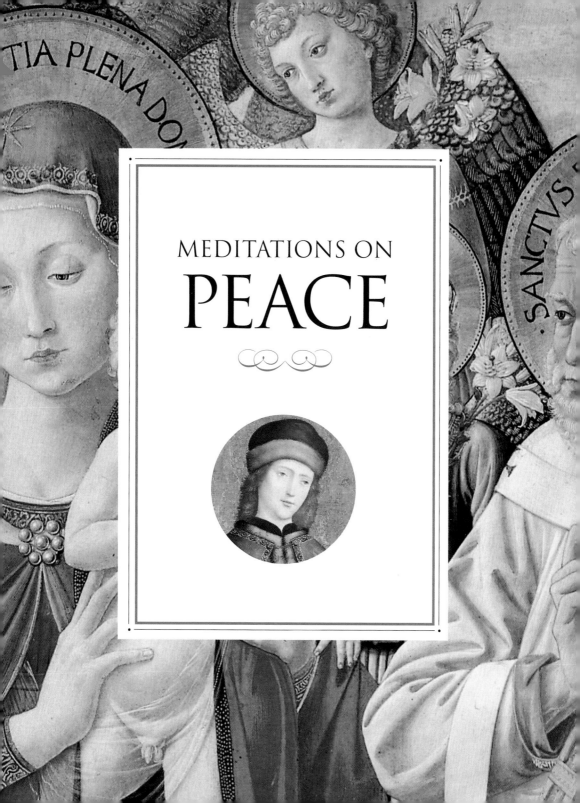

MEDITATIONS ON
PEACE

PEACE IMAGINED

PEACE IS ONE OF OUR deepest needs, but it does not come just for the wishing. Yet even images of it comfort us. Pictures of unspoiled countryside make visual what many people see as the essence of peace. In Constable's *Cornfield* the sun shines, the fruitful fields wait patiently for the reaper, water is sweet and unpolluted, and the animal world is in harmony with the human. Nowhere is there disturbance or annoyance, no raucous noises, no pressures. This is peace as it may appear in our imagination.

The Cornfield, 1826, John Constable
143 x 122 cm (56^1/$_4$ x 48 in), oil on canvas
National Gallery, London

AN IDEAL WORLD

T HE PERFECT COUNTRYSIDE, the wonderful image of peace, is, of course, as imaginary as the perfect city. An unknown artist from Florence saw the ideal city as supremely beautiful and spacious, with large, gracious buildings existing in compatibility. It is a view that uplifts the heart; but the ideal city is uninhabited. Once human beings come onto the scene, with their clutter and noise, this gentle image of peace would be destroyed. But we misunderstand the nature of peace

if we think of it as an ideal world, or as dependent on silence or solitude: we have, sooner or later, to admit reality – with all its in-built anxieties.

Perspective of an Ideal City, c.1470, Unknown Florentine artist
60 x 200 cm (23^1/$_2$ x 78^3/$_4$ in), oil on wood panel
Palazzo Ducale, Urbino

CONDITIONAL PEACE

BELLINI'S ALLEGORIES are not always easy to interpret, but this one clearly has as its theme uncertainty, inconstancy, and insecurity. The globe balances precariously on the woman's knee, and its real support is the child, as likely as all the other children to grow tired of the task and take to frolicking. Any peace that rests upon externals is in such a state of insecurity. A good digestion, no financial trouble, happy relationships, an interesting career: then the world is beautiful to us, the children smile, and we are at peace. But of what value is such a peace? At any moment accident or natural change may disrupt it. A peace dependent on the woman's knee remaining still and the diligence of a small child in persisting in its Atlas-stance is a poor, uncertain peace: we cannot be peaceful in a dependence.

Allegory: Inconstancy, c.1490, Giovanni Bellini
33 x 22 cm (13 x 8¹/₂ in), oil on wood panel
Accademia, Venice

TRANQUILLITY

PEACE THAT DEMANDS unreal conditions is a deception. There is no life without work, anxieties, or tensions. Peace is not found in avoiding these but in understanding them and controlling their force. One of the most tranquil faces in art is Raphael's St Nicholas, an intensely active bishop. The stories about his miracles may be legends, but they attest to his great reputation for practical involvement in the personal distresses of his people. Even here, Raphael shows him, not lost in silent prayer, but reading, with his crozier upright in his hand. The unmistakable inner peace we can see has nothing at all to do with an unstressed life; it comes from his insight into the significance of those stresses, their value and their motivation.

St Nicholas of Bari, (detail from the Ansidei Madonna), 1505, Raphael
209.5 x 148.5 cm (82¹/2 x 58¹/2 in), oil on wood panel
National Gallery, London

A Meaningful Life

WE LONG FOR reassurance, our own personal angelic visit, the removal of obstacles, the certainty of fulfilment. Botticelli's Virgin sways in prayerful wonder as she receives the blessed summons. What will follow? For Mary it will be a life of loneliness and poverty, with her son dying a criminal's death and the only solace her faith. Human strengths can only lead to human satisfactions, and even these are vulnerable to fortune. But these are meagre goals, not enough to lead us into peace. There is no lasting peace that does not rest upon a sense of life's having meaning. For Mary, that meaning was her divine son; for others, it can come from a determination to do what is right, and the solid certainty that this is something that nobody can wrest away from us.

Annunciation, 1489-90, Sandro Botticelli
150 x 156 cm (59 x 61^1/$_2$ in), tempera on wood panel
Uffizi Gallery, Florence

C O N T E M P L A T I O N

PARADOXICALLY, THE WAY to peace is not to seek it, but to seek selflessness. Self-seeking of any kind narrows our potential and destroys the balance on which peace depends. (We must want totality and accept our helplessness to attain it.) Signorelli is not attempting to show us peace in this detail from *The Circumcision*. He is attempting to be truthful, which does not mean naturalistic accuracy but truth to his own vision. In this single-minded pursuit, which leaves no room for the ego, Signorelli has, as an artistic by-product, given us a view of inner peace. These two attendants at the circumcision are not actively involved, but are engrossed in their contemplative role. Their identity is unimportant: in this drama they are onlookers, and they look on with loving concentration. Their peace comes from their response to the actual, unselfconscious and entire.

Two Heads (detail from The Circumcision), c.1491, Luca Signorelli
285.5 x 180 cm (101³/4 x 71 in), oil on wood panel
National Gallery, London

A FLUID STILLNESS

BALANCE IS RARELY mathematical or rigorous. *The Book of Kells* is a celebration of Celtic graphic invention, an intricate marvel of interlace and astonishing complexities. Yet it is even more astonishing in its mysterious balance. It is not a balance of complementaries: the strange human figure at the top right has no counterpart. The page spells out the opening words of St Mark's gospel in Latin, (*Initium evengelii IHU XPI*), and most of the space is devoted to the great verticals of the "N" of the first word. But twist and intertwine as they will, the pattern maintains a stillness, and a purity of balance. Within the movement then, is a deep and satisfying peace.

Opening words of St Mark's Gospel, Book of Kells, c.800
33 x 24 cm (13 x 9 1/2 in), tempera
Trinity College, Dublin

VISUAL PRAYER

THE UNDERSTANDING that peace is the result of an inner balance is what makes this leaf from the Koran so contemplative in its grace. It is written in Kufic script, a wonder of calligraphy, which was created to do due honour to the Word of Allah, and its grand curves, swoops and blotches have an integral harmony peculiar to themselves. The calligrapher has used all his resources – precious ink and artistic sense of patterning – but he has also sought something beyond human resources: a visual prayer, a sacred affirmation of the Holy. Because he has grasped that the objective is beyond human power, the calligrapher has aimed only in the direction of that objective, offering fallibility as a means to achievement; and the miracle has happened.

Leaf from the Koran, (date unknown)
21.5 x 11.5 cm (8¹/2 x 4¹/2 in), ink on paper
Musée Conde, Chantilly

ولقد قالوا كلمة الكفر وكفروا بعد
إسلامهم وهموا بما لم ينالوا وما نقموا
إلا أن أغناهم الله ورسوله من فضله فإن
يتوبوا يك خيرا لهم وإن يتولوا يعذبهم
الله عذابا أليما في الدنيا والآخرة وما لهم
في الأرض من ولي ولا نصير ۝ ومنهم من
عاهد الله لئن آتانا من فضله لنصدقن
ولنكونن من الصالحين ۝ فلما آتاهم من
فضله بخلوا به وتولوا وهم معرضون ۝
فأعقبهم نفاقا في قلوبهم إلى يوم
يلقونه بما أخلفوا الله ما وعدوه وبما
كانوا يكذبون ۝ ألم يعلموا أن الله يعلم

HUMAN FAILURE

WE CANNOT CONTROL our life. If we are set upon doing so, we have abdicated from peace, which must balance what is desired with what is possible. As Hokusai shows so memorably, the great wave is in waiting for any boat. It is unpredictable, as uncontrollable now as it was at the dawn of time. Will the slender boats survive or will they be overwhelmed? The risk is a human constant; it has to be accepted – and laid aside. What we can do, we do. Beyond that, we endure, our endurance framed by a sense of what matters and what does not. The worst is not that we may be overwhelmed by disaster, but to fail to live by principle. Yet we are fallible, and so the real worst, the antithesis of peace, is to refuse to recognise failure and humbly begin again.

The Great Wave, 1831, Katsushika Hokusai
25 x 36 cm (9³/₄ x 14 in), ink on paper
Private collection

COURAGE

GILLES IS A MAN discomforted: he stands exposed, tense, and unhappy. Yet we could not call him a man who is not at peace. Something has happened (Watteau does not spell it out) that has removed him from his fellow actors and left him painfully alone. Gilles is ill at ease, but he has no option: what is happening must be lived through, and he sets himself to do it. This courage – this acceptance of powerlessness and decision to await consequences from which we cannot escape – this is an element of peacefulness. Gilles is at peace because he does not rage against the inevitable. The wisdom is in knowing what is inevitable and what, with courage and intelligence, can be changed. Fundamentally though, nothing matters except to be true to what we know is right.

Gilles, 1721, Jean-Antoine Watteau
184.5 x 149.5 cm (72^1/$_2$ x 59 in), oil on canvas
Musée du Louvre, Paris

THE BLESSING OF PEACE

THERE IS NOTHING passive about peace. Like Crivelli's child, we must always peer around obstacles, never accepting that our vision is limited until we have tried to see to the furthest horizons. We look, we ponder, we revolve possible alternatives. Then, we submit, either to what seems possible or to what seems inevitable. If we have planned with our eyes focused on what is right, then failure is not all that important. It is painful, but it is not destructive. (A child is hardly an image of peace because it does not yet understand the relative insignificance of success or of failure.) The blessing of peace, then, is in knowing that we have only to do what we morally can, and then live without repining in the outcome. Those we love die, possessions are stolen or diminished: only goodness remains. Yet however terrible our suffering, it will not last eternally. On that condition is based our peace.

Detail from The Annunciation, 1486, Carlo Crivelli
207 x 146.5 cm (81¹/2 x 57³/4 in), oil on wood (transferred to canvas)
National Gallery, London

THE ILLUSION OF PEACE

GOOD IS NOT a judgement we can make about ourselves. We instinctively react against Ingres' young Marquis, who so obviously has a high opinion of himself. Whether he considers himself virtuous is not spelt out, but he stands before us with the restrained smirk of self-admiration. Those who are genuinely good, always doubt it. Peace does not depend upon anything, certainly not upon our own certainty of moral righteousness. It depends upon humble desire (with the emphasis on humble) to do what is right. Ingres' sitter, decorations prominent, simplicity of attire elegantly visible, hands electric with a sense of superiority, has a totally dependent kind of peace. Humiliation and failure would explode it, whereas true peace is impervious to events. Peace rests upon the decision always to struggle towards goodness, whatever our condition. In this light, one feels compassion for Amédée-David, with all his spiritual disadvantages.

Amédée-David, Marquis de Pastoret, 1826
Jean-Auguste-Dominique Ingres
103 x 82 cm (40¹/₂ x 32³/₄ in), oil on canvas
Art Institute of Chicago

A BRIGHT FORTRESS

THERE IS AN IMMENSE freedom in peace. Because it needs no external support, it can take all risks that seem wise to it. Pia Stern's *Seaside Residence II* shows a structure, (a "residence") on the very edge of the waves. They surge relentlessly towards it, almost, it seems, engulfing it; yet the structure stands. The unpredictability of the furrowed water, swaying inexorably inward, does not substantially affect the "residence". It is a bright fortress, that apparently exists by other principles. If wild water is black-and-white, then the human home of the spirit is luminous with colour, bright enough to reflect onto the incoming waves, though not to deflect them. Stern shows us two ways of being: the physical, answerable only to accident, to wind and tide; and the spiritual, answerable to an inward sense of truth. One is free-flowing; the other is fixed, grounded in more than its own small compass – in God.

Seaside Residence II, 1994, Pia Stern
21 x 20.5 cm (8¹/₄ x 8 in), pastel on paper
Private collection

CHOOSING PEACE

AN ACCEPTANCE OF the vulnerability on which peace is based, and the weighing up of significance in the light of eternity, can seem to some an abdication from life's everyday realities. Hammershøi's woman sits in an enclosed space, head bent. She could be thought to be imprisoned by her context and weakly complicit with her lack of liberty. Yet the artist shows us door upon door, with a luminous window beyond. Light plays over the woman's form from behind as well as from ahead. If she chooses, she has only to stand erect and move down the waiting corridor. If she stays motionless (reading? sewing?), that is her choice. Peace is never imposed; it cannot be. It is a deliberate choice, an ordering of priorities in a moral context. We look at the options and evaluate them.

Interior, 1908, Vilhelm Hammershøi
79 x 66 cm (31 x 26 in), oil on canvas
Aarhus Kunstmuseum

I SOLATION

THE SAFETY OF PEACE has nothing at all to do with aloofness from other people, keeping oneself free from the risk of emotional pain. Carel Weight's *The Silence* shows three people, almost three generations, motionless, silent, enclosed in their walled space, protected against the outside world and one another. Not one of them is at peace. They sit or stand stiffly, coldly, worryingly remote from family closeness. To isolate oneself is not to be at peace, and makes the acceptance of true life (which peace entails), impossible. Peace does not reject our longings, it is warm, not cold: a passionate commitment to becoming a full person. This means sacrificing the neat goals of the fantasy person, one of which is that it is possible to live fruitfully in hostile isolation from our fellows.

The Silence, 1965, Carel Weight
91.5 x 122 cm (36 x 48 in), oil on board
Royal Academy of Arts, London

JOURNEY TO PEACE

P EACE COMES FROM unselfishly doing what is right. St George has two options: kill the dragon (the rapacity and cruelty within him), or let it ravage. He chooses to kill, and Albert Herbert shows him at the bottom of the picture, vulnerably exposed but triumphant, the deed done. Jonah had no option: the whale engulfed him. His choice then was to lie within its belly until circumstances opened a path to the light. It was not a passive waiting, but a thoughtful one, working out why this had happened and what use he could

St George and the Dragon, Jonah in the Whale,
and the House of God
1990-91, Albert Herbert
66 x 21.5 cm (26 x 8¹/₂ in), oil on wood
Private collection

make of it. The top image, the house of God, exceeds the panel, as if this house can never be confined within man-made boundaries. The house stands open, a rich, bright red visible within. Herbert invites us to identify with the two bystanders: will they enter the solid protection of the house? No moral judgement is made, merely a series of existential possibilities. Peace exists on all three levels.

REDEMPTION

NO IMAGE OF PEACE has ever been more powerful or more encouraging than that of Christ as he faced his passion. He knew that in a short time he would be betrayed by a close friend and that his death would be a terrible one – crucifixion. He would die with his work barely begun, and the sense of failure must have been crushing. He must, too, have felt rejection: why had God, his Father, not protected him? The stained glass painting of this scene is particularly moving, because the thick lead supports, which the glass technically needs, isolate Jesus from comfort, and from his friends lost in sleep around him. He is alone. We are told Jesus was in an agony of grief and fear, yet he was equally in a state of the most profound peace. He did not understand, but he trusted, and would go to death trusting. Peace may not expel terrible emotions, but it underlies them and makes them – as with Christ – redemptive.

The Agony in the Garden, 1441, Hans Acker
104 x 62 cm (41 x 24¹/₂ in), stained glass
The Besserrer Chapel, Ulm Cathedral

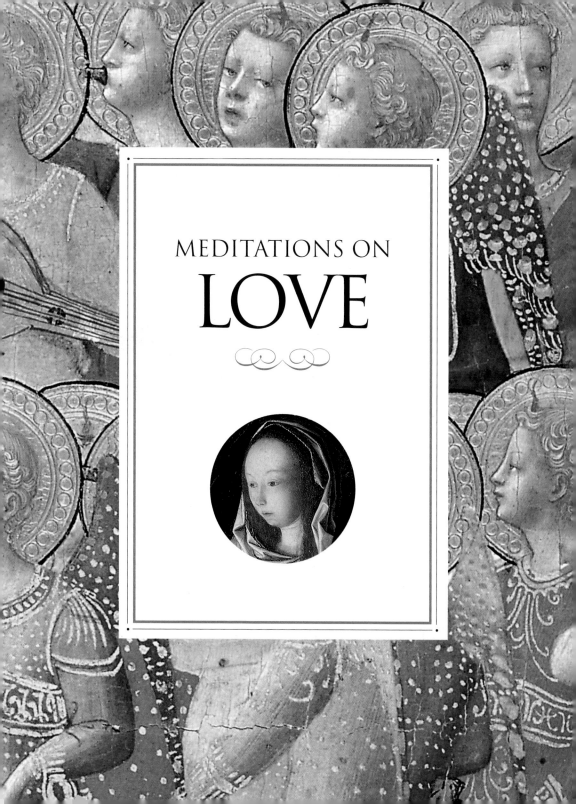

MEDITATIONS ON
LOVE

BODILY EMBRACE

IT IS NOT EASY to say exactly what love is. *The Kiss* might seem a perfect illustration: the passionate emotional and physical involvement of two people. In the intensity of their embrace, Klimt's couple have become one, fused together by their mutual ardour. Is this love? Or is it only the appearance of love? Are they giving to each other, or using each other? Are they concerned with the body as integral to the self, or just the body as an instrument? When they part, the two robed forms withdrawing once again into separateness, will each feel greater reverence for the personality of the other or not? A bodily embrace is very precious, but its real value depends upon what it signifies.

The Kiss, 1907-8, Gustav Klimt
180 x 180 cm (71 x 71 in), oil on canvas
Österreichische Galerie, Vienna

TENDER REVERENCE

REVERENCE IS THE deepest form of respect. A serious desire to recognise another as important in his or her own right. It accepts that we are not central to the universe. It is this attitude of tender humility that Rembrandt expresses with such power in *The Jewish Bride*. His couple are not in their first youth, or beautiful in any classic sense, but both are infinitely moving in their expression. We know at once that they love each other. Each gives love and receives it. Love is supremely beautiful, but like the golden chain the man has placed around the neck of his beloved, it also binds. Each is surrendering freedom, but willingly so, thus facing the truth that we cannot have everything; if we love, we make a delimiting choice. They do not even need to look into each other's eyes. Rather, they ponder with wonder, the implications of their blessedness and the meaning of total commitment.

The Jewish Bride (detail), 1665-7, Rembrandt Van Rijn
166.5 x 121.5 cm (65^1/2 x 48 in), oil on canvas
Rijksmuseum, Amsterdam

CHOOSING LOVE

IKING COMES EASILY: it is spontaneous. Real love, that which will last and make an essential personal difference, is always difficult. It is a matter of choice, either at the beginning or later. At some stage, we have to face up to the seriousness of love. Lárusdóttir's couple are stumpy and unappealing average humanity. He is not merely offering flowers: her hesitation, and the presence of the grandfather clock with its insistence on time, emphasises that it is himself that he is offering. The wistful onlookers drive the message home: they are those who escape the wonder and the pain of love. The woman looks inward: will she embark upon this relationship, the most absolute of which a human being is capable? He thrusts life towards her, an almost threatening presence. The choice is still open: he has cast his lot, she has not.

Karólína Lárusdóttir, 1993, Man Gives Woman Flowers
35 x 45 cm (14 x 18¹/2 in), oil on canvas
Private collection

LIFELONG FIDELITY

THE ARNOLFINI WEDDING PORTRAIT is full of symbols of
marriage: from the dog, emblem of fidelity, to the fruit
and the bed, symbols of fertilty (though history records
no children in this marriage). But at its centre is the solemn
moment in which the young man pauses before placing his
hand over that of his girl bride, accepting her as his wife. The
discarded shoes and lit candle tell us this is a holy ceremony:
each is tremulously aware of the other, devoutly intent on the
seriousness of their action. They are making an absolute decision,
a mutual undertaking. They know
what they are doing: accepting the
gift of a lifelong companionship,
offering as much as they receive.

The Arnolfini Marriage, 1434, Jan van Eyck
82 x 60 cm (32¹/₄ x 23¹/₂ in), oil on wood panel
National Gallery, London

MOTHER LOVE

LOVE IS BOTH INFINITELY REWARDING and endlessly demanding. The two aspects are inseparable. The mother in Berthe Morisot's picture is her sister Edma, rapt in thought as she gazes at her baby daughter. In having a child, parents undertake an unbreakable relationship. As Morisot shows it, the mother's part in this relationship is all gift. She can receive nothing as yet from the child, who is too young to respond. The mother has the duty to protect and cherish, and the alacrity with which it is carried out does not disguise that it is a burden. Edma is not free; her time now belongs to her child. But it is a burden of love, and this mother seems to feel only contentment in her servitude.

The Cradle (cropped), 1872, Berthe Morisot
56 x 46 cm (22 x 18 in), oil on canvas
Musée d'Orsay, Paris

THE LESSON

THE TREE EXUBERATES in blossom, the cabbages are thick on the ground. Van Gogh's young parents concentrate on the work of love: teaching their child to walk. Love is essentially active, intent upon the needs of the other, and the rough intensity of Van Gogh's clumsy forms expresses the dedication of the parents. Spade and wheelbarrow stand idle and forgotten; both parents are conscious of nothing but the needs of their child. The fruitfulness of the setting is highly appropriate: the child is the fruit of love, and the parents' work is bringing the child to maturity. Not only the child: we become aware that the slender and youthful pair are themselves maturing as they unite in this activity. The child seems to like its lesson, but that is not the point. Love must be able to say No as well as Yes, and even to seem unloving if, in the end, that is for the other's betterment.

The First Steps (after Millet), 1890, Vincent van Gogh
72 x 91 cm (28¹/2 x 36 in), oil on canvas
Metropolitan Museum of Art, New York

CHASING THE BUTTERFLY

PARENTAL LOVE is potentially its purest form, and may be the most painful. Gainsborough, whose marriage was unhappy, adored his two daughters, whom he called Molly and the Captain. Their mother's flawed psyche was inherited by both girls, and their father agonised over them all his life. Neither was to know happiness, and his many pictures of them show a sad fore-knowledge of this. To leave those we love their independence, to accept that we cannot make their choices for them, that they cannot live by our hard-earned experience: this is part of love. We have to allow those dear to us to chase the butterfly, however convinced we are that it is uncatchable. We can never give the butterfly of happiness to another: each must catch it alone. For some, it will be ever elusive, and love must work within that painful understanding.

Chasing the Butterfly, c.1755-6, Thomas Gainsborough
114 x 105 cm (44³/4 x 41¹/4 in), oil on canvas
National Gallery, London

THE GAZE OF LOVE

I F LOVE EXISTS UNDER ALL CIRCUMSTANCES, then so do the objects of love. There is always beauty to be found. It may not be for our possessing, but learning detachment is part of respect. The world is there despite us yet, and if we are not

greedy, it is there *for* us. Zurbarán sets four vessels in a row; he lets the sun shine on them. He gazes in awe at their simple elegance, captivated by the sheer actuality of their shapes, by the shadows they cast, and the play of light on their colouring.

He makes no statement; he simply delights, and gives thanks. Because of his reverence, Zurbarán allows the magic visible to him to become apparent to our eyes too. Love communicates.

Still Life, 1635
Francisco de Zurbarán
46 x 84 cm (18 x 33 in)
oil on canvas
Museo del Prado, Madrid

PARTING

ALL LOVE, whether of child, parent, partner, friend, even of place, possession, or animal, is potential of suffering, because of death. We cannot possess or hold fast anything or anyone: it is all gift. Life contains inevitable partings, and inescapable pain. The loveless are protected against this suffering: the zombie feels nothing. We are alive in proportion to our response to love, and our pain at parting is in proportion to the extent of that love. Altdorfer's leave-taking is a wonderfully unsentimental depiction of what it means to say goodbye. He glorifies none of his characters: Mary has enormous feet, thrust almost violently upon the viewer's attention. Christ and his disciples are ready to move out into a world of possibilities; his mother and her companion women must stay, imprisoned in the decay of their old environment. For them, the sun is setting: Christ is aware of it, compassionate yet still resolute. It is his vocation to go, and though his mother grieves, so it has to be. The deeper the love, the deeper its pain.

Christ Taking Leave of His Mother, c.1520, Albrecht Altdorfer
141 x 111 cm (54 x 43¹/2 in), oil on wood panel
National Gallery, London

REGRET

NONE OF US can claim a perfect record in love. We all fail and betray, even inadvertently. This is perhaps the worst pain of love, failure for which we feel culpable. The Magdalen, having come to love Christ after a life of selfishness, grieved forever after. Donatello shows her in old age, his fragile wooden carving furrowed with the marks of her long penance. She is literally abraded to the bone by sadness for what might have been, and yet her beauty is still luminous with hope for what is still to come. This is a vision of what all love knows: repentance for inadequacy.

The Magdalen, 1453-55, Donatello
185 cm (73 in), gilt and painted wood
Museo dell'Opera del Duomo, Florence

CONDITIONAL LOVE

PERHAPS THE MOST enduring failure in love is that of not revealing one's true self. The temptation to seem better than one is, not to risk the rejection truth might bring, is a perpetual one. We need great faith in the reality of love to dare to present ourselves in naked trust to the person we love. This brightly attired young man shows us the beguiling charm of his gesture. But he carries a bird that is caged: if we conceal our true selves before love, then we keep the bird safe only in confinement. Open the cage, and the bird can truly live.

Chelsea porcelain, 1759
18.5 cm (7 in), porcelain
Private collection

ABSOLUTE TRUST

THERE CAN BE NO LOVE without trust, yet it must be an intelligent trust. Love is not blind, despite the saying, and we cannot truly give our hearts to the unknown. The story of Abraham and his only son Isaac has always been a daunting one. Abraham believed that God was calling him to sacrifice his son, and he was saved from this hideous action only at the last minute. I have a personal reading of this story: to me the only one that makes sense. It is that God would never ask us to do something that is evil, and Abraham must have known this. So what we have is two gigantic acts of trust, each based upon knowledge of the other person, and of God. Abraham could only have gone ahead in the absolute belief that the horror would never happen. Isaac, for his part, submitted to being bound and laid on the altar, believing against all appearances that his father would not harm him. If Abraham had not known God: if Isaac had not known his father, such trust would have been madness. Love insists that we make a true judgement and then cleave to it, whatever the appearances.

Sacrifice of Abraham, 1994, Albert Herbert
20 x 20.5 cm (7³/4 x 8 in), oil on zinc
Private collection

O BSESSION

LOVE CAN BE MISDIRECTED. If we choose, we can fix our hearts unavailingly. Narcissus fell in love with himself. He pined to death, longing for a response that of its nature could not come: it was his own reflection he was courting. Echo fell in love with him, despite the evidence that he had no eyes for anyone but himself. She faded to a voice on the breeze, and he to a flower. As Poussin shows it, she is already dematerialising, unable or unwilling to accept reality. Beautiful Narcissus is visibly losing strength as he yearns for the self he sees in the waters. Poussin makes no judgement: but he reveals both as passive. True love (Cupid with his torch) lingers regretfully in the background. Love in itself is alive and active.

Echo and Narcissus, c.1628-30, Nicolas Poussin
74 x 100 cm (29 x 39¹/2 in), oil on canvas
Musée du Louvre, Paris

BEYOND THE CAVE

ARTHUR BOYD TAKES the myth of Narcissus and sets it in the contemporary Australian landscape. Yet it could be an archetypal landscape, a nowhere place of sand and sea and distant scrub. Narcissus is enclosed in the dragon cave of his own mind. Boyd suggests another reading of the myth, the passion for self-knowledge. Narcissus seems to be seeking not so much his self, in an egoistic sense, as insight *into* self, something wholly different and worthy of dedication. Yet it is outside the confines of his cave that the orange tree blooms: love requires selflessness. Narcissus squats as he paws the pool, stiff with anxious desire. He even seems to lose his humanness, a reflected tail bestialising him. Whatever the motive, love must range abroad – not be confined to the self. The whole world is there for loving, but we must venture outside ourselves to discover it.

Cave, Narcissus, and Orange Tree, 1976, Arthur Boyd
152 x 122 cm (60 x 48 in), oil on board
Savill Galleries, Sydney

THE FORTRESS

HOWEVER HAZARDOUS the development of love may be, love itself is a certain blessing. To love means to put someone or something before oneself, to rise above the pettiness of the ego, and in that we can never go amiss. Ken Kiff shows a very bleak world indeed. The sky is the darkest black, and even the moon or sun is a clouded ball. In its occluded

illumination we can make out a shrivelled tree, as stark as seaweed, and beside it a pale rock. In this arid world, a flower lifts up its leaves in a gesture of rejoicing. Its petals glow with sweet vitality: whatever else is dead here, this small bloom is joyfully and brightly alive. Love, in fact, cannot be extinguished. No black sky or dying trees can affect its inner radiance.

Flower and Black Sky 1987-88
Ken Kiff
18 x 44 cm
(7 x 17 1/4 in)
water-colour
Marlborough Fine Art, London

FORGETTING SELF

IT IS EXTREMELY difficult to love unselfishly. We aspire to it, because the moment we subordinate the other's needs to our own, the moment we use them, we have, for that moment, ceased to love. Being selfish, a user, and regretting it, overcoming it, starting again; this is one of life's patterns. Death of a beloved can be an acid test; we are being abandoned, even if unintentionally. Utter concentration on the other in such a time of crisis is very rare. That is what makes Monet's picture so extraordinary. Camille was his wife, her early death left Monet not only bereft of her companionship but with small children now fully dependent on him. Obviously, Monet is to some extent escaping the pain by externalising it, but it is, nonetheless, a remarkable act of egoless activity. He forgets himself in catching the least glimmer of light on his wife's face. In itself, this self-forgetfulness is the essence of true commitment.

Camille on Her Deathbed, 1879, Claude Monet
90 x 68 cm (35¹/2 x 26³/4 in), oil on canvas
Musée d'Orsay, Paris

PERFECT LOVE

PERFECT LOVE MAKES NO DEMANDS and seeks nothing for itself. This extraordinary and beautiful carving of Christ and St John shows us that there is no such thing as right and wrong love, since, for it to be love at all, the other's happiness comes first.

St John Resting on the Bosom of Christ, early 14th century
Master Heinrich of Constance
141 cm (55½ in), wood
Mayer Van den Bergh Museum, Antwerp

SYMBOL OF LOVE

IN THE END, love is to be practised rather than written out. Howard Hodgkin's *Fruit* does not attempt to paint a real fruit, but rather to recall and to celebrate the thing that has given such delight. It is a tiny picture, with several layerings of rich red border, but the remembered fruit escapes the confines, over-whelming in its richness and glory. He is painting remembered intensity, choosing it as his theme, forgetting himself in appreciation of it. This is the perfect symbol of what it is to love.

Fruit, 1988-89, Howard Hodgkin
32.5 x 40.5 cm (13 x 16 in), oil on wood
Private collection

MEDITATIONS ON
JOY

THE NATURE OF JOY

JOY IS NOT a constant condition. Most people manage a settled cheerfulness, but this, however admirable, has nothing to do with joy, which flashes suddenly upon our darkness. Like the lightning in El Greco's *View of Toledo*, joy not merely illuminates our interior landscape but transforms it. The world becomes different, marvellous, and unique.

View of Toledo, 1600, El Greco
121.5 x 108.5 cm (47³/4 x 42³/4 in), oil on canvas
Metropolitan Museum of Art, New York

CHOOSING JOY

RUBENS IS CONSUMMATELY the painter of happiness. But this sunlit, unreflecting sense of well-being, precious though it is, is not joy. Joy is something deeper, and in a sense sterner. Although we cannot command it, we choose joy, making a deliberate commitment to happiness (essentially another word for peace). Rubens delights in the positive: the rainbow symbolising hope (and in itself so beautiful), the light glinting on the rich meadows, the benign cattle and their fruitful surroundings. Yet there are dark elements, too, in the picture if we want to seek them out: the sunless woods are not far away. Rubens chooses: he emphasises the good things. Joy is independent of choosing: it overwhelms and suffuses us.

Rainbow Landscape, c 1636, Peter Paul Rubens
136.5 x 236.5 cm (53³/4 x 93 in), oil on wood panel
Wallace Collection, London

PASSING PLEASURE

PLEASURE, LIKE JOY, comes unbidden (though rarely unsought), but it is of its nature infinitely less than joy. Bonnard's wonderful *The Table* is a depiction of pure pleasure. He has dwelt lovingly on every element, especially the radiance of light, and rejoiced in it. But it is too earth-bound to be a picture of joy. It is a snatched moment of sensuous celebration, of food, wine, sunlight, beloved woman; but it is transient, and this sense of the passing adds to the pleasure. Joy, however, lasts, if only in its effects.

The Table, 1925, Pierre Bonnard
103 x 74 cm (40^1/2 x 29^1/4 in), oil on canvas
Tate Gallery, London

JOY IN INFANCY

THE VERY SMALL CHILD, who is loved and protected, knowing nothing of the hazards of life, may know unreflecting joy. The anonymous American painter who saw this baby in Pennsylvania has painted a child enclosed and vulnerable, but wholly confident in love. The half-smile, the folded hands, the head resting on the over-sized pillow: together these show one of the marks of joy: its absolute belief in what is experienced.

Baby in Red Chair, c.1810-30, Unknown artist
56 x 38 cm (22 x 15 in), oil on canvas
Abby Aldrich Rockefeller Folk Art Center
Colonial Williamsburg Foundation, Williamsburg, Virginia

EMBRACING JOY

WE SURRENDER TO JOY: we have no option. Margaret Neve's girl dances in the moon-light, resting upon the silky air as the great moon rests on the soft waters. She throws her arms out wide as if to float backwards, held up by pure joy. This gesture of embrace, opening as widely and welcomingly as is possible, marks the experience. Joy is felt as profoundly "right", as what "ought to be". In grief, part of the pain comes from our feeling that we should not suffer so – that it is fundamentally alien to our being, this even though we all suffer, and frequently. Yet we reject suffering as a basic human truth, while greeting joy as integral to our very substance.

By Moonlight, Margaret Neve, 1994
23 x 28 cm (9 x 11 in), oil on wood panel
Montpelier Sandelson, London

INSPIRATION

JOY DOES NOT NEED any specific cause or reason. It can come about through the lowliest of objects just as through the noblest. Redon looked upon this sea shell, and it is as though he was swept into an insight of the nature of the universe. There on the ocean floor, without light or spectator, the shell is luminous with its own strange beauty. Redon may have seen this only in his imagination, but that is a valid way of seeing: it reveals truth, rather than fact. This weirdly lovely artifice of nature is a proclamation of the universal ubiquity of joy.

The Shell, 1912, Odilon Redon
51 x 58 cm (20^1/$_2$ x 22^3/$_4$ in), pastel
Musée d'Orsay, Paris

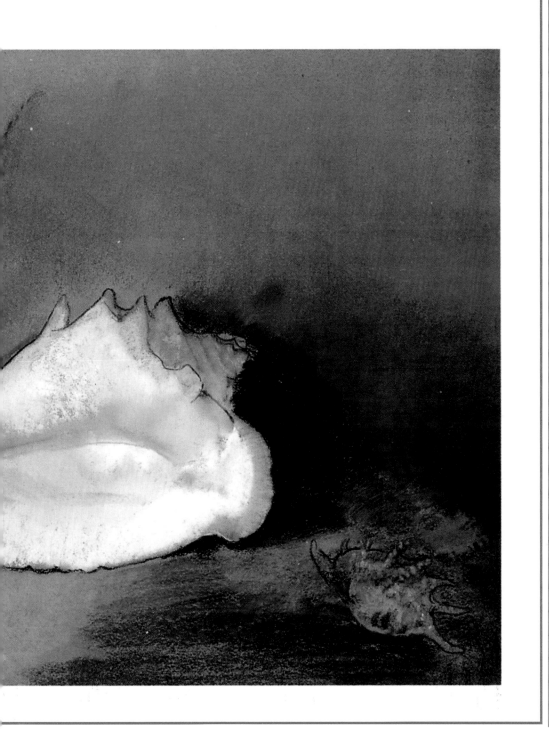

SALVATION

AS WELL AS SEEMING profoundly right, a revelation of the meaning of life, joy also comes as absolute gift. It cannot be won or deserved. Da Fabriano's St Nicholas swoops down on the desperate sailors, most of whom have not even seen him yet. The sails have split and the sailors are furiously jettisoning their cargo, unaware that salvation is miraculously

St Nicolas Saves a Ship From the Storm, 1425, Gentile da Fabriano
30 x 62 cm (12 x 24¹/2 in), tempera on wood panel
Vatican Museums

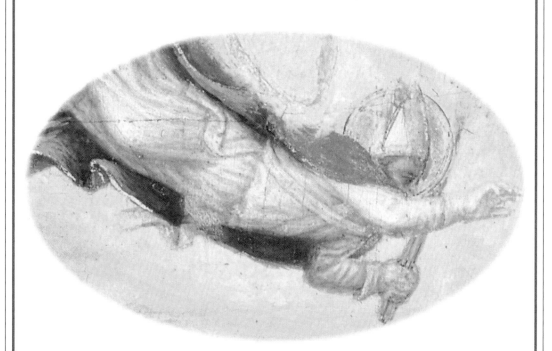

at hand. We are shown the moment before joy, the precise instant
when despair and horror will be transformed into the wonder of
their rescue. It is unforeseen, a gift. Out of the blue – literally –
joy comes exultantly upon them. What joy seems to do is to
establish us so securely in itself, and in the remembrance of its
presence, that we can cope with whatever life has to throw at us.

A Vision

THE EXPERIENCE of joy leaves behind it an awareness of our personal freedom. Windows have opened for us onto a vision that we cannot possess at will, but which – having experienced pure joy – we now know exists; and the windows remain open, even if we must, for the present, stay within. Dufy's double windows reveal the richness of the distant world, its gleaming possibilities, its actuality. The space we occupy may be as in the painting, cluttered and even oppressive, but after joy it is no longer imprisoning. We have glimpsed something greater, something of liberating power, and there are no external obstructions to our movement out of limitation and into that freedom.

Interior with Open Window, 1928, Raoul Dufy
66 x 82 cm (26 x 32¹/₄ in), oil on canvas
Galerie Daniel Malingue, Paris

LOST IN TIME

THE WAY INTO blessed freedom may be not to live in too great a dependence on the passage of time, on the inexorable approach of tomorrow and mortality. The sense of joy in Renoir's *Children on the Sea-shore* seems to flow from the timelessness of their experience. It is not a real world, with its softly coloured pastel background made up of a blur of bathers, and with the children themselves half melted into their context of colour. They are responsive only to the immediacy of their sun-filled leisure. We feel that this holiday will be recalled, in the future, as joy, though perhaps not yet fully realised as such.

Children on the Sea-shore, Guernsey, 1883?, Auguste Renoir
91.5 x 66.5 cm (36 x 26 in), oil on canvas
Museum of Fine Arts, Boston

R A P T U R E

APTURE, HOWEVER SHORT LIVED, is a concomitant of joy. It is not a precise equivalent, since ecstasy is as much piercing pain as it is joyfulness, yet joy partakes of rapture in that its touch always draws us forcibly out of the confines of self. (The word means seizure, a strong carrying-away.) Since the face of St Teresa displays this dual character of ecstasy, an almost unbearable intensity, we might look rather at the face of the angel. His face is lit with the wondering expression of selfless joy. It is not his ecstasy; he is merely the instrument. He is excluded from St Teresa's divine intimacies, yet he watches her with total delight, lost in the happiness of believing what is not his to possess.

Ecstasy of St Teresa, 1645-52, Gianlorenzo Bernini
350 cm (114 in), marble
Santa Maria della Vittoria, Rome

WELL-SPRING OF JOY

THE GREAT MATISSE had a very hard time as a young artist, and it must have seemed an act of madness to spend his wife's dowry on a small Cézanne painting of three female bathers. Yet Matisse claimed that in all times of despair he had

looked at this tiny talisman and received hope from it. It was a well-spring of joy to him, refreshing and restoring his flagging confidence. *Bathers* is a mysterious work, growing in power the more we contemplate it. Cézanne exorcised his fear of women by painting them: here his women appear gross, unappealing, yet somehow vulnerable. They are exceptionally clumsy figures, held in the picture's centre by two diagonal tree trunks, motionless beneath a mellow sun. Cézanne could control the uncontrollable in his art, and that wonderful sense of innocent power is what gives the *Bathers* its immensely satisfying quality. Cézanne was painting his joy, imagined if not experienced, and Matisse drew it from him by a sort of osmosis. It is equally there for us.

Bathers, c.1879-82, Paul Cézanne
55 x 52 cm (21³/4 x 20¹/2 in), oil on canvas
Musée du Petit Palais, Paris

TRIUMPHANT JOY

FOR MANY PEOPLE life is a struggle. At its worst, it is a struggle to survive, at its best, a struggle to become totally true. In its essence, joy celebrates triumph. But it is not victorious over others, or over the world; it takes no account of hostility. Joy, in itself, is victorious over defeat; for in that joy-filled moment, and forever after in memory, we have risen above the struggle and entered into victory. Joy assures us that it will most certainly *be* victory, and it allows us to taste of it beforehand. Flanagan's *Drummer*, a wildly exuberant hare, is a comic yet apt emblem of this triumph.

*The Drummer, 1989-90
Barry Flanagan
244 cm (96 in), bronze
Yorkshire Sculpture Park*

INWARD CONTENT

THIS DELICATE PORCELAIN dancer is unaware of any audience. She dances for her own delight, lost in a dream of inward content. It is this quality of being lost, of sweet oblivion to all else but what happens within her, that makes this a sculptural expression of joy. Nothing can guarantee us joy, or coerce its presence. But for many people, music is an occasion when joy is likely to choose to visit us. Her movements are guided, not only by the conscious will, but by all-absorbing rapture.

Shepherdess, 18th c, Meissen
17.75 cm (7 in), porcelain
Private collection

JOYFUL CONFIDENCE

WHEN JOY TOUCHES us it can seem a godlike experience, suddenly making us aware of the eternal, assuring us that we have nothing to fear, and that the foundation of all Being is Love. Like *Diana the Huntress*, we stride out uncluttered through the morning sunlight. We need no covering for our feet: they are met by tender grass and flowers. We need no clothing, since in the world where joy has led us, there is no need for concealment. We may go naked and unashamed, accepted for what we are. Outside of joy, it takes very great trust in another to appear without protection, but here, there is only vigorous and unencumbered movement forwards. The dog – our animal nature – springs obediently beside the virgin goddess, our spirit. Diana does not even need to look where she is going: in joy there are no mistakes.

Diana the Huntress, c.1550, School of Fontainebleau
132 x 191 cm (52 x 75 in), oil on canvas
Musée du Louvre, Paris

RADIANT TRUTH

WHATEVER THE TITLE of this painting, Craigie Aitchison makes it clear to us that these are not real grapes in a real bowl. The saturated colour, so dazzlingly bright, affirms that this is the artist's world, where grapes hang suspended in perfect roundness against a clear scarlet

Pink Bowl with Grapes, 1992, Craigie Aitchison
30.5 x 35.5 cm (12 x 14 in), oil on canvas
Thomas Gibson Fine Art Ltd, London

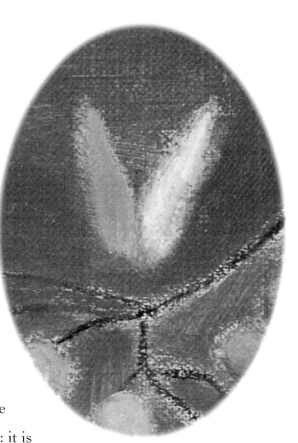

background, and where a two-coloured butterfly hovers exquisite in the centre. This is so radiant a picture, so intense in its certainties, that it seems to have, as its real, hidden theme, the absolute-ness of joy. There are no half-measures here: it is the all-or-nothing that joy reveals to us. There may be a dull brown lower layer, but it is held firmly in its place, at the bottom, sat upon by brightness. Only when overwhelmed by joy do we know, in our very bodies that this is the truth of it.

BEYOND EXPERIENCE

I T IS INADEQUATE, even misleading, to speak of "experiencing joy", though it is impossible to find another phrase that can suggest what is meant. Joy is too great to be experienced. It is never our own, never within our power. It is rather that we are taken up into its vastness, and that what we experience is not joy itself but its residue: our reactions, our emotions, after the vision has left us. Monet's *White Clematis* says something of this, if only in its impression of a vision too vast for his encompassing. The blazing whiteness, with the shimmer of purest lemon yellow at the heart, spills out and beyond the artist's canvas. We feel that no canvas, however large, can capture what is seen. In the most literal sense, this is a painting of a vision; we recognise it, not for what it is, but for what it makes us recall.

White Clematis, 1887, Claude Monet
92 x 52 cm (36¹/4 x 20¹/2 in), oil on canvas
Musée Marmottan, Paris

REALM OF BLISS

ALL ABSTRACT ART is different, and it is pointless to generalize. But there is a certain strain that consistently reappears, where the artist seems to be painting from pure bliss. Hambleton's *Ascent* shows two parts of a richly coloured circle, rayed with light, too vast for the canvas. Ruthlessly bisecting these segments is a rectangle, a whiteness flecked with covert and secret forms, half-luminous, half-obscure. The rectangle rises and then is abruptly curtailed as the canvas finishes. Yet, somehow, the ascent continues, "out there", in that real world to which joy gives us temporary entrance.

Ascent, 1987, Mary Hambleton
38 x 45.5 cm (15 x 18 in), oil on canvas
Pamela Auchincloss Gallery

JOY AND PRAYER

JOY IS PRAYER EXPERIENCED, or to put it another way, joy gives us the bliss of actually feeling the reality into which prayer can draw us. We *see* truth in joy, receive it in prayer. Both are valid forms of the same truth. Prayer demands faith and fidelity, and we prove our desire for these by our actions; but we do not need any actions to receive joy. It is a shortcut, but as in prayer, it is how we apply to our lives what we are shown that matters. Borgognone's saint is now seeing for herself what she believed in all her life. It may be the weaker spirits who, for their faith, need the encouragement of joy; saints can live in the bare reality of joy, without the need actually to feel its wonder.

Studies for the Ascension of a Saint, 1675-79, Borgognone
42 x 27.5 cm (16¹/2 x 10³/4 in), chalk on paper
Kunstmuseum, Düsseldorf

LIFE-AFFIRMING JOY

KLEE DIED RELATIVELY YOUNG, slowly withering away, and his style changed as the inevitability of death became inescapable. *Death and Fire* is one of his last works, in which the German word for death, Tod, forms the skull's features (and is repeated several times in the painting). An apocalyptic sun like a great doomed ball sits low on a horizon, held aloft by Death, like a gruesome trophy. The man who approaches is stripped to his essence: is he humanity moving steadily towards the grave? All this might seem sombre, yet the painting is aglow with the most life affirming-colour. The death's head is an intensely luminous form, set in a context of gold, green, purple, and above, the deep red of fire. With great seriousness, Klee announces that death is a purifier, like fire, and a means to fulfilment. This is the most terrible, seen as the most beautiful. This is the real power of joy, to make us certain that, beneath all grief, the most fundamental of realities is joy itself.

Death and Fire, 1940, Paul Klee
46 x 44 cm (18 x 17¹/₄ in), oil on burlap
Kunstmuseum, Berne

INDEX

PICTURE CREDITS

p1 Reproduced by courtesy of the Trustees of the National Gallery, London

p3 Reproduced by courtesy of the Trustees of the National Gallery, London

p5 Musée d'Orsay, Paris

MEDITATIONS ON SILENCE

p6-7 Reproduced by courtesy of the Trustees of the National Gallery, London

p7 Reproduced by courtesy of the Trustees of the National Gallery, London

p9 The Metropolitan Museum of Art, Bequest of Benjamin Altman, 1913 (14.40.622) ©1991 By The Metropolitan Museum of Art

p11 Palazzo Pitti, Florence/ Bridgeman Art Library

p13 Private Collection

p15 Metropolitan Museum of Art, New York/Giraudon

pp16-17 Courtesy of the artist

p19 Reproduced by courtesy of the Trustees of the National Gallery, London

p21 Courtesy of the artist

pp22-23 Reproduced by courtesy of the Trustees of the National Gallery, London

pp24-25 Courtesy of Jill George Gallery, London

p27 Courtesy of Thomas Gibson Fine Art Ltd

pp28-29 Besançon (France), Musée des Beaux-Arts et d'Archéologie. Cliché Ch. Choffet

p31 Alte Pinakothek, Munich/ Joachim Blauel - Artothek

pp32-33 Collection Haags Gemeentemuseum - The Hague/©1995 ABC/ Mondrian Estate/Holtzman Trust. Licensed by ILP

p35 Courtesy of Edward Totah Gallery

p37 Uffizi Gallery, Florence/Scala

pp38-39 Kunsthistorisches Museum, Vienna

p41 Staatliche Museen zu Berlin, Preußicher Kulturbesitz Nationalgalerie

p42 By Courtesy of the Board of Trustees of the Victoria and Albert Museum

p43 Courtesy of Alistair Sampson Ltd

MEDITATIONS ON PEACE

p44-45 Reproduced by courtesy of the Trustees of the National Gallery, London

p45 Reproduced by courtesy of the Trustees of the National Gallery, London

p47 Reproduced by courtesy of the Trustees of the National Gallery, London

pp48-49 Palazzo Ducale, Urbino/Scala

p51 Accademia, Venice/Scala

p53 Reproduced by courtesy of the Trustees of the National Gallery, London

pp54-55 Uffizi Gallery, Florence/Scala